This Temple

poems by

K. Nicole Wilson

Finishing Line Press
Georgetown, Kentucky

This Temple

*In memory of Rane Arroyo
who encouraged me to know every flame.*

Copyright © 2016 by K. Nicole Wilson
ISBN 978-1-63534-065-5 First Edition
All rights reserved under International and Pan-American Copyright Conventions.
No part of this book may be reproduced in any manner whatsoever without written permission from the publisher, except in the case of brief quotations embodied in critical articles and reviews.

ACKNOWLEDGMENTS

"Unfinished Work" in *Open Windows*
"Sharp Edges" in *Marginalia*
"Eve was the Original Catcher" in *Circe's Lament*
"Severance" from Lexington Poetry Month (2014) Blog via Accents Publishing

Publisher: Leah Maines

Editor: Christen Kincaid

Cover Art: K. Nicole Wilson

Author Photo: Zannah Reed

Cover Design: Elizabeth Maines

Printed in the USA on acid-free paper.
Order online: www.finishinglinepress.com
          also available on amazon.com

Author inquiries and mail orders:
Finishing Line Press
P. O. Box 1626
Georgetown, Kentucky 40324
U. S. A.

Table of Contents

Take the Heart 1

Unfinished Work 2

Vascular Thrombosis 3

September Letters 6

Disimile 8

Sharp Edges 9

Eve was the Original Catcher 11

I Crumple the Paper 12

Fabled Creature 13

Rhyme of the Red Balloon 15

Inside Story 16

Severance 17

Bluegrass Burial 19

At the Temple 20

"For the eyeing of my scars, there is a charge."

Sylvia Plath, "Lady Lazarus"

Take the Heart

grate on paper,
drain every bloody drip of detail,
align splattered designs with a sharpened scraper,
see the omens in the entrails.

Drain every bloody drip of detail,
feel the organ's final pulsation,
see the omens in the entrails,
the air's rich with coppery inhalations,

feel the organ's final pulsation
as red hands squeeze the end note,
the air's rich with coppery inhalations,
but it's the iron taste that'll stick in the throat.

As red hands squeeze the end note,
the poem's almost ready for plating,
but it's the iron taste that'll stick in the throat.
Share grace before the meal, or start meditating,

the poem's almost ready for plating,
everyone with a steak knife salivates for art.
Share grace before the meal, or start meditating,
pass to the left, take the heart,

everyone with a steak knife salivates for art.
Align splattered designs with a sharpened scraper,
pass to the left, take the heart.
Grate on paper.

Unfinished Work

> *How soon hath Time, the subtle thief of youth,*
> *Stol'n on his wing my three and twentieth year!*
> John Milton, "Sonnet VII"

Writing in the dark I imagine I am Milton,
but with minimal sight so I need not recite
    books to daughters unborn,

in my twenty-third year I begin to wonder
if my best lines really do lie behind the coming times,

I do not have the poet's dead eyes,
but a swollen, purple arm paints sign of clot in my vein,

I open my mouth and swallow the pill,
pinch the skin on my belly, thrust eleven needles through,

thunder storms on my stomach,
fear rises like the morning, warming,

will my pen begin a line again?
Will all the unborn daughters never hear me sing?

Vascular Thrombosis

i.

Each tiny pain,
every flashing thought,
am I unraveled and insane
due to one small knot?

Every flashing thought,
constant pinch of vein,
due to one small knot,
unblottable stain.

Constant pinch of vein,
arm purple, garish.
Unblottable stain.
Magnificent blemish.

Arm purple, garish,
an incongruent nightmare,
magnificent blemish,
continuous scare.

An incongruent nightmare,
am I unraveled and insane?
Continuous scare,
each tiny pain.

ii.

Each tiny pain brings a flash of fractured thought,
urging the dissection of every little ache.
I'm unwinding, insane, from an unusual knot.

The first Doppler scan claimed no sign of blood clot,
which is a mistake technicians often make
—each tiny pain brings a flash of fractured thought.

Reinspection reveals the elusive spot,
demands I take notice of every little ache,
I'm unwinding, insane, in an unusual knot.

Regress back to nightmares. Watch the body rot.
Replay vivid reminders of what's at stake,
each tiny pain brings a flash of fractured thought.

Inject eleven anticoagulation shots,
eat rat poison—how many pills can I take?
I'm unwinding, insane from an unusual knot.

Maybe one day I'll know what this low tide taught
(try to go with the flow), but every little ache,
each tiny pain, brings a flash of fractured thought.
I'm unwinding, insane. In an unusual knot.

iii.

Each tiny pain inspires fearful flashes of thought,
I prepare to meet Death with every little ache,
my arm oozing with the purple of paranoia
still an inch thicker than the right, thanks to the clot
—jot down any possible symptom—make no mistake,
if anything's writer's block it's hypochondria,

even the word's quite a serious occlusion
damming the fragile, blue tributaries of heart.
I flounder in the interruption of conscious stream
and demand a life of better circulation,
each new exhalation is the perfect place to start
deciphering if the body whispers or screams,

but what if briefly ignoring pain proved the difference,
truly, what is this temple without proper defense?

September Letters

Angry announcement:
Boston Planes Blasted as Bombs!

Carefully, they crashed,

catastrophe
descends,
debris drops onto downtown,

evil escapes
efficient and almost
flawless, but for four fighting men
(gratitude given at gravesites)

history hands out heavy
information, but
it's more than I can take.

Jump! The flames are too hot.
Jump! There are no arms to catch you and
Kentucky is just next door,

lost, little ones cry,
life leaves, lifts into the skyline.

Monday was quiet, but
murder made its mark on Tuesday,
mourning
now we need news that
night comes for only so long,

oceans object and owls cry,
omens
predicting interrupted peace,

please pray
quietly or with bold
quilts of red, blue, black, and gray,

read and heal, tomorrow
rests in the cup of your hands.

Sorrow sounds a symphony,
sweeps us inside a song,
a tale of twins collapsing in terror.

Take my hand
until we can walk
under stars and feel safe again,

visions explode and
visions explode and

varying strategies divide our vitality
when we should have
waged our first wars for healing.

Xeroxed copies flash repetitious
X-rated horror films on CNN, do you know
yesterday's forgotten by desensitization?

Yell *yes* for freedom after
zooming jets
zipped life closed.

Disimile

> *"Her body a bulb in the cold and too dumb to think ...*
> *The bees are flying. They taste the spring."*
> *Sylvia Plath, "Wintering"*

The poet is nothing like her poems,
polished rhyme framed with white,
pertinent lists, discovered maxims,
each word left is right.

Polished rhyme framed with white,
meter sleek, rhythm strong,
each word left is right,
no hidden barbs or prongs,

meter sleek and rhythm strong,
a constant spring unfurling,
no hidden barbs or prongs,
no sharp points like a bee's sting,

a constant spring unfurling,
no continuous thunderstorms.
No sharp points like a bee's sting,
they are perfect, practiced forms,

no continuous thunderstorms,
pertinent lists, discovered maxims,
they are perfect, practiced forms,
the poet is nothing like her poems.

Sharp Edges

> *Yeah you got a piece of me,*
> *but it's just a little piece of me,*
> *and I don't need anyone.*
>   Adam Duritz, "Have You Seen Me Lately?"

When I collected my hair as if for ponytail, I must have thought
by the time long red strands grew back
to that same luscious length, there would be no lines left
from the falls I shared with him,
falls like September towers and fading leaves, our descent,
sudden severances, like the foot of red locks in my hand,

when he raged again into our room, I held up my hand,
he never told me what he thought,
but the look on his face was enough, its quick descent,
O of realization, anger at what he couldn't get back,
tears fell next, but I had no sympathy for him—
I should've waited with the scissors until after he'd left.

The next day a stylist tamed the shards of what was left,
I told the story: my identity falling as trash from my hand,
leaving out parts like trying to call the police on him,
the phone, fragments in the parking lot
   (but what she must have thought!),
she asked if he stayed, if I took him back,
said I was brave. My head shook polite dissent.

I fell for him in the Red River Gorge, a blind descent,
fast like two a.m. Gray's Arch repellers, the world left
behind, and I never wanted to go back,
fear forgotten, gloves to prevent rope burn big on my hands,
because of Half Moon Rock I didn't give second thought
to warnings co-workers gave, looks people threw him.

Of course they were right to tell me to avoid him,
but rationalizations ripped from my lips in rapid dissent,
I didn't care what anyone thought,
and there were so many times I should have left—
made him go instead—instead of taking scissors in my hands
and sundering strawberry waves, warm waterfall down my back,

but I kept going back,
until forced to live in a hotel to hide from him
after coming home from work to find my room
    wrecked by his hand,
pieces of computer glass, picture frames, scattered markings
    of forced descent,
I took some trinkets from the past, but the bed we shared I left,
there was no more need for thought,

and when I look back I don't care what he thought,
only see him picking through trash for the dead hair I left,
holding it in his hands, winding curls into a jar:
    token of our descent.

Eve was the Original Catcher

Licking chocolate off the sharp edges of a serrated knife
is worth the risk,
it's better to eat cake than be a wife,
guarding the plate like Carlton Fisk

is worth the risk.
If the pitching's distressed,
guarding the plate like Carlton Fisk
is useless,

if the pitching's distressed,
cleaning the dish
is useless—
a dustless world is just a wish.

Cleaning the dish
leaves time for contemplation:
a dustless world is just a wish,
total happiness is an imagination,

leave time for contemplation,
don't obsess,
total happiness is an imagination,
try to minimize the mess,

don't obsess,
it's better to eat cake than be a wife.
Try to minimize the mess,
licking chocolate off the sharp edges of a serrated knife.

I Crumple the Paper

and like Jordan at the line, I close my eyes
and fire at the hoop, since there's no need to look
at the made shot, I can turn back to the book,
number for fourteen new lines, and then improvise:
I am Solomon and infinitely wise.

Back up, revise. Heat the oven before you cook.

Beautiful Muse why hast thou forsaken me?
I search for your presence all possible places,
but you've vanished—like Mike transforming to Air,
I open bottles, but no sustenance swims there,
I open windows to proclaim your praises,
but my notes lack luster, and fall hollow, empty.

I survey the mass of white wads with contempt,
knowing none are worth the ink or field goal attempt.

Fabled Creature

Once upon a time
he called me
a unicorn,

though
he never
told me himself
(with words),

but our friend did, later,
after intimate, mythical months
had passed.

Now our friends say I'm socks
he grabs
when his limbs grow
lonely with cold,

they worry aloud
that I'm a nail
drowning in wood,

as vital to him
as one of the chopped and flaming logs
breaking into embers

in his fireplace at night—

sweet smoke lifting to my lungs
each time my shoes
set soles on his drive

—until I finally read
the fairy tale as false,

and can say,

I am this poem,
and finished.

Rhyme of the Red Balloon

Feel the embrace of lips into words,
birds that soar through blue—hue of lost love are you

—Do you hear me red balloon?
So soon you've left.

Theft! My dawns take flight
and night falls from stormy clouds.

LOUD is the thunder.
The lightning that struck the string, fierce.

Pierce my heart as you fly away,
day will never rise again to my eyes,

so I'll wait here in listless state,
anticipating a return that can never be true.

The mate of the broken line tied like a bracelet
in a knot around my wrist.

Inside Story

I'm great on paper.
Please don't drop by,
the view's a re-shaper,
you'll say goodbye.

Please don't drop by,
if you read the stacks of unedited lines
you'll say goodbye,
you'll leave me behind closed blinds,

if you read the stacks of unedited lines
—my stitched and bloody body of work—
you'll leave me behind closed blinds,
visiting unlit corners where demons lurk.

My stitched and bloody body of work,
clarity compared to my cluttered brain.
Visiting unlit corners where demons lurk,
I sing a melancholy refrain,

clarity compared to my cluttered brain,
the view's a re-shaper.
I sing a melancholy refrain,
I'm great on paper.

Severance

The saddest thing
in my refrigerator
is not the emptiness
of the glass shelves
that fog when I linger
with the door open

contemplating the nothing.

Nor is it the assorted crumbs,
tiny death mounds
for dinners past, meals shared,
top shelf remains at rest
next to Coca-Cola cans that gleam
with a slight sheen

of condensation.

Certainly, the best thing
encased in the temperature-controlled cold
are the cherries in the crisper drawer,
cherries from my visit home,
cherries filled with savory juice,
and pink, delicious flesh,

pink on my fingers and lips.

Not even the thing
I'm calling *the science experiment*
that's growing in the porcelain crock pot,
a thing that was once the makings
for nachos, just like the nachos
I made for my housewarming party,

for which you were the first to arrive.

Not even the two beers by the light
with your name on them
are as sad as the champagne
we never got to at New Year's,
sitting in the lowest corner

in unbottled celebration.

Bluegrass Burial

I fly home the anniversary of my grandmother's death,
on the plane I bring a novel that singes me with its ink,
marks me like the infinite psalm stitched like coal onto my back,
I'm heading home to the rolling hills, the family I lack—
kin who're covered with winter on *Priney* Lane, or at the brink
of sinking—I think of sweet Southern winds with every thin breath.

Circulation skips through some rungs in the ladders of our blood,
Ma-maw's heart dropping pace, slowing ever slightly for ten years,
and I'll never forget my arm, knotted, ugly with vein's clot,
left forever darker than the right, purple like springtime buds,
purple and splotchy like my face, streaky from funeral tears,
liquid lining my jaw's edge, miming prayer at the new year's plot.

My parents and I, we share few words, just pack my apartment,
boxes for storage, the souvenirs of how my light's been spent.

At the Temple

The new year rings cold,
the new year begins alone,
and the furnace will not hold,
valves frozen and still as stone.

The new year begins alone
in empty, icy chambers,
valves frozen and still as stone,
just a hearth of ash, no embers,

in empty, icy chambers
the chimney shares nothing with the world
just a hearth of ash, no embers,
bare floors shine frosty and pearled,

the chimney shares nothing with the world,
because there's nothing to burn but paper,
bare floors shine frosty and pearled,
at the heart there's not one warm vapor,

because there's nothing to burn but paper,
and the furnace will not hold,
at the heart there's not one warm vapor.
The new year rings cold.

K. Nicole Wilson grew up on the baseball fields and basketball courts of Maysville, KY, and reading year-round in its public and school libraries. While attending the University of Kentucky, the right brain won and the poet emerged from the shell of mathematics major. Nurtured under the kind and discerning eyes of Leatha Kendrick, James Baker Hall, and Nikky Finney, it became clear there was no other choice. K. Nicole earned her MFA in poetry at Spalding University's brief residency program, studying and blossoming beneath the brilliant Greg Pape, Richard Cecil, Molly Peacock, Barbara Hamby, and Rane Arroyo. It was Rane who told her not to be afraid to be tender; these are some of those poems.

During graduate school she lived in the Rocky Mountains of Colorado, reading Stephen King, and shouting poetry from snow-capped peaks. The distance from her Kentucky home gave new insight to K. Nicole's writing, creating a pining. A move to shrouded Seattle confirmed the need to go back to the Bluegrass, back to a city where it actually rains more: Lexington, the state's beating blue heart. She hibernates in a little harbour with Oy, her beautiful billy-bumbler/cow dog where they root for Wildcats and waggle as much as possible.

www.ingramcontent.com/pod-product-compliance
Lightning Source LLC
LaVergne TN
LVHW041524070426
835507LV00013B/1814